T0381392

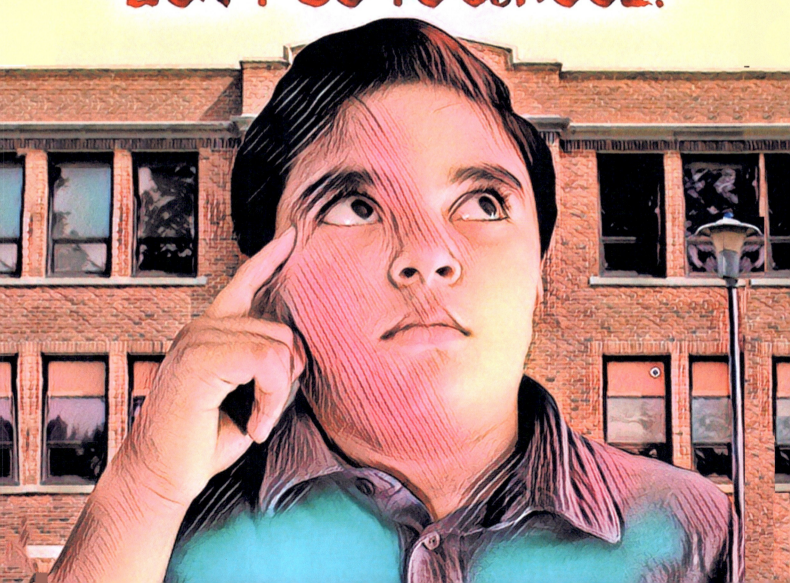

AuthorHouse™
1663 Liberty Drive
Bloomington, IN 47403
www.authorhouse.com
Phone: 1 (800) 839-8640

Published by AuthorHouse 03/22/2019

ISBN: 978-1-7283-0534-9 (sc)
ISBN: 978-1-7283-0535-6 (e)

Print information available on the last page.

Any people depicted in stock imagery provided by Getty Images are models,
and such images are being used for illustrative purposes only.
Certain stock imagery © Getty Images.

This book is printed on acid-free paper.

authorHOUSE®

This is a story of a brother and sister, twins, who lived in New York City. Both of their parents were working, but then their mother lost her job, and that made it difficult financially for the family. The parents decided that the children's mother would homeschool them while the father was on the road for days at a time driving a truck.

It seemed that the children and mother were doing well with homeschooling; they enjoyed the flexibility, but they missed their father when he was away for days at a time; they missed going places with him.

2

The children told their father they wanted to spend more time with him, but he told them that he had to work to earn the money the family required. The parents convinced the kids that unless the mother found a job, the father couldn't quit his job as a long-distance trucker.

The boy said, "You told me that I'm a big boy, so I'm old enough to work."

But his mom told him that he was still a little kid and not old enough to work. The father told his son and wife that the boy could work just to avoid the argument.

The next day, after the father had left for work, the boy told his mom that he wanted to find a job, but she said he had to wait until his father came home to find out what job would be best for the boy.

The kids made a plan. They usually played in the park while their mother took a nap after their homeschooling lessons, so they decided that would be a good time for the brother to sneak out to find a job.

The next day when the kids were playing in the park, the sister said to her twin brother, "Don't go too far. Cover yourself or put on sunscreen, and don't get dirty. The most important thing is that you put whatever you earn safely in your pocket, and make sure you come home as soon as you finish your work. I'll wait for you on the steps outside our house."

He walked to the other end of the park, but he didn't know how to cross the road. He had to wait for someone to help him cross. He saw an older woman pushing a shopping cart full of grocery bags. He noticed she was having difficulty pushing the cart over the uneven sidewalk. The boy approached her and offered to help push the cart.

The old woman said, "Sure, my child, I would love that. Thank you. You came to me just like an angel at this difficult time."

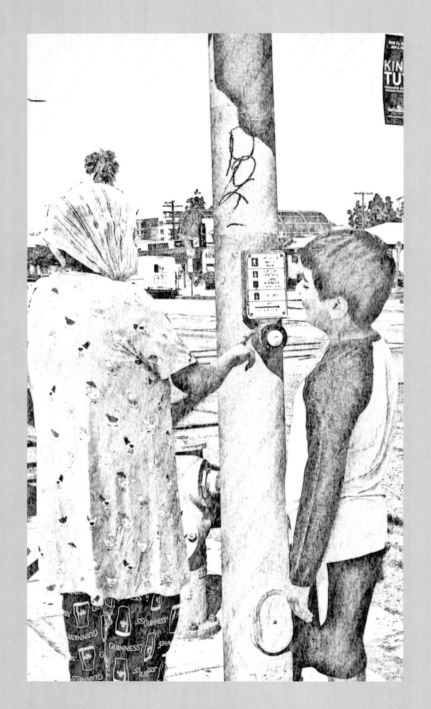

The boy started pushing the shopping cart, and the woman pushed the walk button on the pole. She told him they could cross when the signal started flashing. They walked a couple of blocks and got to her huge house, and she invited him in.

The boy saw many pets and lots of toys lying around. He stayed with her for a while to chat and play with her pets. Then the boy told her that he needed to go home because his sister was waiting for him. Before the boy stepped out of her house, the woman offered him an ice cream in a wrapper.

He took the ice cream and stepped out. He opened it and was about to take a bite, but then he remembered that his sister had told him he should put whatever he earned into his pocket and take it to her. So the boy put the ice cream carefully in his pocket and headed home.

When he approached his house, his sister started laughing at him because the ice cream had melted in his pocket. Then she scolded him for getting messy.

He told her all about the old woman and the ice cream. He said, "Don't act like Mom. I did what you told me—I put what I got in my pocket."

They laughed and went inside.

They cleaned themselves up as they always did after playing at the park and before their mother got up from her nap. After that, it was time for them to study. Their mother got up and started preparing dinner.

The next day, both kids woke up early, made their beds, and went to the bathroom to brush their teeth and take showers. They dressed and went to the table for breakfast.

"Mom, we're hungry, and we're ready to eat!" the daughter said.

Their mom was preparing breakfast. "I'm not late you kids are early. You guys woke up early today."

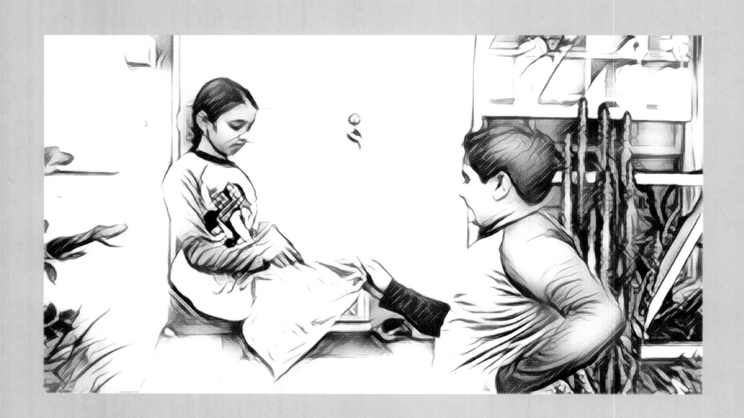

After breakfast, they started their studies, and a couple of hours later, it was time to play at the park. The sister said to her brother, "After work, put whatever you get in this bag, and don't spend time playing—you need to come straight home to me."

He remembered that the woman had asked him to come whenever he wanted to, so he decided to go to her house. She was happy to see him since she lived alone and nobody came to visit her. After the boy played with her guinea pig for a couple of hours, the woman realized he was very fond of the guinea pig. When he was ready to go home, she handed him the guinea pig and told him that he could have it because she was too old to take care of it. He thanked her and took the animal.

Once he was outside, he put the guinea pig in the plastic bag his sister had given him as per her instructions. On his way home, the animal chewed its way through the plastic and jumped out. The boy saw it escape. He tried to catch it, but the guinea pig disappeared into the bushes. The boy looked and looked, but it was no use. It was gone! The boy had gotten his clothes dirty from crawling in the bushes.

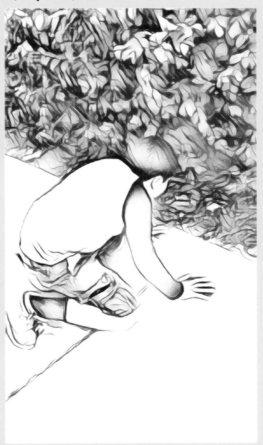

He got home carrying the torn plastic bag and explained to his sister all that had happened.

His sister was a little disappointed, but to cheer him up, she said, "Don't worry, brother. I will think of something better for tomorrow. You need to take a shower and change your clothes before Mom gets up and sees you."

On the third day, the kids went to play at the park again, but that time, she asked him to play a little bit with her before he left because sitting on the steps alone was boring. "If you play with me, I'll give you my idea," she said.

After playing on the swing for a little while, the boy wanted to find some work to do. He asked his sister, "What advice do you have for me today?"

She smiled and said, "Whatever you get today, hold it gently in your arms."

The boy said, "Thank you so much," and he left.

He went again to the woman's house, and she invited him in. Her parrot said to him, "Hey angel boy!" The boy stretched out his hand, and the parrot flew over and landed on his hand gladly. He started to play with the bird.

"How did you teach the parrot to speak?" the boy asked the woman.

"This parrot is smart," she said. "Do you like it?"

"Yes I do!" said the boy.

As the boy left that day, she handed him the cage with the parrot.

He thanked her and started to walk away. His thoughts went back to what his sister had told himthat he should hold whatever he got that day gently in his arms. He opened the cage and tried to hold the bird, but the parrot got free of the boy's hand and flew up to the woman's roof. The boy saw no way to retrieve it, so he went home.

He got home; his sister was not waiting for him on the steps. He saw that the door had been left ajar. He quietly crept into his room. His sister was in his room making a box. She looked up and saw her brother. She asked, "What did you get? Is it outside?"

She ran to the door, and he followed her. When she didn't find anything outside, she realized that her brother might have messed up again. He told her what had happened.

The sister was disappointed again, but she said, "Hope sustains life. Don't worry. Better luck next time. I'll think of a better idea tomorrow."

They went to the kitchen to get something to drink.

After they had taken showers, they studied some more.

In the morning after breakfast, they started their homeschool classes and activities. After lunch, they and their mother went to the pool for swimming lessons. After an hour of that, they went home. The kids asked their mother if they could go to the park.

The mother replied, "You can go, but make sure you don't get your clothes dirty. I have noticed that you keep getting your clothes very dirty."

The kids replied, "Okay, Mom!"

The girl asked, "Mother, can I take my jump rope to the park?"

"Yes you can," she said, "but don't jump together at the same time or you'll get hurt. If you want, I can go with you to the park."

The son replied, "No, Mom, we'll be fine. You can take your nap. We will be okay."

The children went to the park and played on the slides for a while. He asked his sister if he could go to work.

She said, "I knew you were going to ask me that. That's why I came prepared with this rope."

The boy said, "Rope? I don't like to jump rope. I just want to go to work. Do you have any ideas for me today?"

"Yes I do, my dear brother."

"Hurry up and tell me what it is. I'm curious."

She said, "Whatever you get today, tie it with this rope."

The boy thanked her sister.

"Please come home as soon as you can. It seems that time stops when I am waiting for you."

"Don't worry about me. I will meet you at home," he yelled back.

The boy got to the old woman's home and saw her sitting on her front porch. "Hello! How are you today?" he asked.

She said, "Much better now, angel, now that you're here!"

They spoke for a while, and then they went inside. He spent some time playing with the toys in her house. He wondered why she had so many toys when she didn't have any kids there.

When it was time for him to leave, she gave him the scooter he had been playing with, and he thanked her. He sat on the scooter thinking he would ride it all the way home, but then he remembered his sister had given him the jump rope to tie it up with. He tied the rope over the handles of the scooter so he could pull it home. The scooter was heavy, though, and he got blisters on his hands from trying to pull it, so he decided leave it in front her driveway.

His sister was waiting for him outside their home and saw that he was empty-handed. He told his sister what had happened with the scooter, and she said, "Don't worry. You have one more day tomorrow. Dad will be home tomorrow night. Hopefully, you will be successful tomorrow. Let me take care of your blisters."

She put some ice on his blisters, and that made the boy's throbbing hands feel better. After dinner, they went to bed early so they would have enough rest for their test the next day.

The kids woke up early and started to review their work for the test. Mother called them for breakfast and told them, "Someone will be coming today to assess you guys on all you have learned this far."

Later that day, after the testing was over and the visitor had left, the kids went out to a karate class with their mom, and they had some ice cream on the way home. They changed out of their karate clothes and asked their mom what they had been waiting all day to ask her if they could go to the park for a little while.

Their mom replied, "I don't think you can go today because we are expecting your dad to come any time now."

The kids said, "Mom, dad will come much later. He always gets home in the evenings since he start his driving job."

They pleaded with their mother, and she finally decided to let them go to the park.

The son said, "Mom, you can take your nap while we are playing."

Mom replied, "Not today. I have to prepare dinner and do many chores before Dad arrives."

The children left for the park. On the way to the park, the boy said, "I can't play with you today, sis. We don't have enough time. Mom wants us back soon."

"I get so bored being by myself," she said.

"This will be the last day I go to work. Do you have any suggestion for me today?"

"Yes I do," she said. "Whatever you get today, sit on it."

"Okay, thanks. I won't disappoint you today."

He left for the old woman's house. When he got there, he saw that she had a visitor. He walked in curious to learn who the visitor was because the woman never had visitors. The old woman introduced the visitor to the boy. "This is the angel I told you about," she told her visitor. She turned to the boy and said, "This is my attorney."

They greeted each other. After a little conversation, he said he needed to go back soon because his father was coming home that day.

The old woman gave him her dog and told the boy, "You can keep the dog for a day or two while I'm out of town with my attorney to handle some important paperwork."

The boy was so excited about taking the dog home. He thanked the old woman.

As soon as he stepped off her porch with the dog, he remembered what his sister had told him to do—sit on whatever he got that day. He tried sitting on the dog, but it scooted forward, and the boy fell and scraped his elbows and knees. The dog ran around the house into the backyard.

The boy went home, and his sister was waiting for him anxiously. She was concerned when she saw that he was limping and had scrapes on his elbow and knees.

He told her what had happened at the old woman's place. They snuck into their room, where his sister cleaned and bandaged his scrapes.

A moment later, the doorbell rang. Mom called out, "Kids, open the door. It's Dad!" but they did not hear her. The mother called out a few more times, but they still did not hear her, so she answered the door. It was her husband, who asked, "Where are the kids?"

She replied, "In their room."

They went to their children's room and were astonished to see their daughter bandaging their son.

The father took his son to the doctor's office accompanied by his wife and daughter. On the way, the girl confessed to her parents about what had happened the last five days since their dad had gone to work. The parents were very mad at their kids.

They told the doctor that the boy had injured himself when he fell off a dog. That made the doctor laugh. He told the parents that homeschooling was not for every child and that if they could, they should send their children to a regular school.

"Kids are not only getting an education in school," he said. "They are also learning how to work with and socialize with their peers. Even the president's kids go to school. If they wanted, they could afford the best tutors in world, but they choose not to because they want their children to socialize and interact with people from different cultures. From age one to five, children's brains develop. Your son lacks presence of mind; if he went to a regular school, he would have thought logically and not have followed his sister's advice."

The moral of the story is this: every child has the right to go to school, and we encourage that. We know that parents are their children's best and first teachers, but their children get so much more than just an education at school. They learn to be punctual, responsible, respectful, and well behaved, and they learn how to communicate with and learn from one another.